WATERS

Edith Newlin Chase

Ron Broda

Scholastic Canada Ltd.

Toronto New York London Auckland Sydney
Mexico City New Delhi Hong Kong Buenos Aires

Sprinkling, wrinkling,
softly tinkling,

twinkling tiny brook,

running, funning,
hiding, sunning,

cunning baby brook,

joins a grown-up brook.

Dashing, splashing,
sunlight flashing,
stony grown-up brook,

13

joins the river,
broad smooth river,

deep as deep can be.

Slower, slower, slower flowing,

wider, wider, wider growing,

till it empties all its waters out
into the great huge sea.

Rolling, rolling,
tossing, rolling,

splashing waves forever rolling
in the great wide sea.

To Lyra and Larsson,
Michael and Isobel,
and other children who love
streams and the sea.
E.N.C

For my brothers and sisters:
Bob, Tom, Terry, Connie, Crystal,
Fred, Kevin, Kim, Todd and Brigit.
Also in loving memory of our father,
Fred Broda.
R.B.

Photography by William Kuryluk.
The illustrations for this book were done with paper
sculpture and watercolour. Each layer was cut, formed
and painted before being glued into place.

No part of this publication may be reproduced or stored in a retrieval
system, or transmitted in any form or by any means, electronic, mechanical,
recording, or otherwise, without permission of the publisher,
Scholastic Canada Ltd., 604 King Street West, Toronto, Ontario, M5V 1E1,
Canada. In the case of photocopying or other reprographic copying, a
licence must be obtained from Access Copyright (Canadian Copyright
Licensing Agency), 1 Yonge Street, Suite 800, Toronto, Ontario M5E 1E5
(1-800-893-5777).

National Library of Canada Cataloguing in Publication Data
Chase, Edith Newlin
Waters

Poems

ISBN 0-545-99416-0

I. Water—Juvenile poetry. 2. Children's poetry,
American. I. Broda, Ron. II. Title.
II. Title

PZ8.3.C358Wa 1994   j811'.54   C94-930928-1

ISBN-10 0-545-99416-0 / ISBN-13 978-0-545-99416-3

8 7 6 5 4   Printed in Singapore   07 08 09 10